Angel Messages from the Beyond

Angel Messages from Beyond

The Complete Book of...

Juan Nakamura

Translated by ...

Angel Messages from Beyond

The Complete Books of Answers

Juan Nakamori

Translated by Akiko Fujinami

RIDER

LONDON · SYDNEY · AUCKLAND · JOHANNESBURG

First published in 2006 by Rider, an imprint of Ebury Publishing, Random House, 20 Vauxhall Bridge Road, London SW1V 2SA

Random House Australia (Pty) Limited
20 Alfred Street, Milsons Point, Sydney, New South Wales 2061, Australia

Random House New Zealand Limited
18 Poland Road, Glenfield, Auckland 10, New Zealand

Random House South Africa (Pty) Limited
Isle of Houghton, Corner Boundary Road & Carse O'Gowrie Houghton 2198, South Africa

The Random House Group Limited Reg. No. 954009

Papers used by Rider are natural, recyclable products made from wood grown in sustainable forests.

Printed and bound in Great Britain by Mackays of Chatham plc, Kent
A CIP catalogue record for this book is available from the British Library

ISBN 1846040388 (until Jan 07)

ISBN 9781846040382

Preface

Angels come from other realms, beyond the earthly plane. One of their purposes is to help us and to care for us in times of trouble, or simply to point out how best we can use our time on Earth. Whatever your question or your problem, insight and guidance are yours for the asking. The Angels are there, waiting for you to reach out to them so that they can inspire you with their heavenly wisdom.

———✣✣✣———

The pages in this book contain 82 celestial messages that have been specially channelled for you from the angelic realms that lie beyond this dimension. Some of the messages are long and some are short. All are powerful. Read them carefully and consider them well.

How to Awaken Your Inner Angel

To discover the message that the Angels have for you at this moment, simply do the following:

* Hold the closed book, shut your eyes and focus on your breathing.

* Gradually calm your thoughts and, as you relax, focus on your question or problem.

* Send your question out into the Universe and wait.

* Whichever number between 1 and 82 first comes to you, go to that message and study it carefully. This is your answer.

Angel
Messages

Praise all aspects of yourself.

Being alive is, of itself, praiseworthy.

If you always fret about your weak points and your faults,

Your good points and strengths will diminish in radiance.

You were born into this world with blessings.

Appreciate and praise every aspect of yourself.

Your situation is itself a
message for you.

It shows what you think, feel and
believe in.

If you earnestly seek to know
yourself,

Every situation will prompt your
spiritual growth.

Love yourself in the same way that God loves you.

Every person is born to learn and practise love.

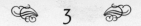 **3**

You possess within yourself rich talents bestowed on you by Heaven.

Become aware of this, and accept that latent talents

Reside deep within you.

The qualities you like about yourself constitute your genius.

The qualities others praise in you constitute your genius.

If you keep ignoring or rejecting this,
it will stay buried within.

If you appreciate it, respect it and
keep nurturing it,

Your genius will shine like a brilliant
jewel.

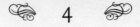

4

A smile

Outshines any jewels,

And enhances your beauty

More than anything else.

Have you ever considered

How much charm and power

One smile can have for others?

Wherever and always,

You possess a wonderful gift

That you can offer to those
around you.

Remember –

Fill your smile to the brim

With love from your heart.

Begin by practising your best smile

By yourself in a mirror

Every morning.

There may be some mornings

When you are so
disheartened,

And find it difficult.

Still,

For your own sake,

Begin your day

With a beautiful gift of
encouragement: ⁓

A smile for yourself.

Even if your smile may not be

Rewarded with a smile from others,

Never mind.

Instead,

Believe in the charm and power of the smile.

True happiness belongs

To those

Who can offer a heartfelt smile

To any person

At any time.

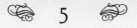

5

'To live'

Is

'To know your True Self'.

You will never be able to live another's
life,

Nor

Can anyone else live
your life

For you.

And yet, in order to live,

You must know your
True Self.

If you wish to live in true
happiness,

You must live,

Not for the sake of

Your parents, family, friends,
your teacher or lover,

Nor for

Society, school, your workmates
or the outside world,

But,

For your own True Self

In heart and soul.

This is the basis of 'perfect happiness'.

It means doing what you truly
want to do.

Instead of trying to make do
haphazardly or for the time being,

Clearly and firmly engrave in your
mind

What you want to achieve – your
dreams and goals.

The key is to believe

In fruitful results and, with gratitude,

To rise to the challenge with joy and
enthusiasm.

To know your True Self

Requires courage, effort, responsibility,

Open-mindedness and thoughtfulness.

In order to live 'true' to your self,

You must tune your body and mind
into

The great Source of life.

6

Do you allow yourself

To feel things freely?

Feeling is beyond all logic.

Isn't it often the case that,

Before you allow any feeling

To take hold of you,

You start to analyse

What you should be feeling –

How to feel

Rightly,

Effectively,

Perfectly,

And

Ideally?

If you ask

' What is the best way to feel?'

The answer is

'Simply to feel.'

Calmly observe

Which feelings

Your heart and body

Are savouring

This very moment.

For,

Whatever they are,

Your own feelings

Are the best means

By which to know your own truth.

Feeling is

Personal and unique.

It is free and,

Most importantly,

It is that which you cannot
ask another

To experience on your behalf,

Nor can you learn how to feel from
someone else.

If you open yourself to your feelings,

Guidance from the great Source of life

Will come to you naturally

In the form of feelings.

7

Live with an open door
to your mind.

When you fear something, or avoid
something,

You may find it difficult

To open your mind.

Remember, though,

That the things that come to you

Through that open door

Are

Only those things that you need,

Only those with which you can cope,

Only those that can afford you
freedom.

And,

By allowing yourself to receive,

You will experience the joy of
nurturing love.

True love does not choose its object.

The boundary of true love is immeasurable.

We all live to realise this goal.

Now, like a small child,

Open your mind,

And

Be true to yourself

Just as you are.

Even if you take only one or two steps
at a time,

Learn to relish the joy of climbing

The rainbow-coloured stairs that
stretch towards Heaven,

The first step of which

Is

To open your mind.

You are connected to all things by love.

If you are able to forgive yourself, you are also able to forgive all things.

Within the whole, you exist,

Within yourself, exists the whole.

You are animated by all things.

To love yourself is to love the whole.

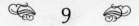

You invite the people you need
into your life.

Each encounter contains an
important meaning:

Pleasant people, kind people,
amusing people,

Nervous people, stubborn people,
self-obsessed people.

In order to know yourself, you will
continue to meet people

And, through relating with them,

You will be able to improve every
aspect of yourself.

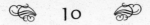

10

You are not merely a body that becomes tired or ill.

Your original nature lies in Eternal Life

That is not bound to any shape nor has an end.

Clothed in a robe called the physical body,

You create your life in this world.

You are a traveller who has visited this
Earth many times.

Your original nature, which is a soul,

Moves, loves and learns through your
physical body.

There is nothing in this world

That is not worth

Cherishing.

Beautiful things, ugly things, petty things,

New things, outdated things,

Praise that feels pleasant to the ear,

Good news, health or illness,

Hard work, the kind-hearted and even
the egotistical:

All are to be cherished.

From that which can be touched
and seen

To the intangible and the invisible,

If you relate to every person,
to every thing

And to every situation that arises in
your life

Resolutely and with a cherishing mind,

All will become precious, valuable and worthy.

Instead of disliking, running away from, and hating;

Instead of ignoring, criticising, and despising;

If you observe calmly from a broader perspective,

You will begin to see all things
differently.

True meaning – that which has been
hidden until now

Will then be revealed to you.

Because, when you see through the
mind's eye of your True Self,

Whatever is no longer necessary
for you

Will no longer bother you,

———— ❧ ————

And will disappear from your sight.

Through cherishing the people, things and situations in your life,

You cherish and nurture your True Self.

12

In this vast Universe,

Nothing exists accidentally.

There exists only

The perfect Law of the Universe,

And

Love, freedom and energy.

With all that has been
given to you,

You have the means to think freely,
feel freely, and

Create freely.

And yet,

You are also given the freedom

To believe, 'I have nothing!'

But beware:

Such a thought may attract

A situation in which you truly have nothing.

If you choose to believe

'Indeed, I am blessed',

You will attract all that you need

With which to create the reality that you aspire to.

Your thoughts, words and actions

Contain an enormous power.

Therefore,

If you keep on worrying,

You will, as a result, attract reasons to be worried;

And,

If you allow yourself to be happy,

You will attract happy events to you.

There is no accidental incident or chance encounter.

Acknowledge your potential.

Every single moment represents a fresh
opportunity

To attract a whole new world to you.

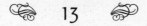

13

When you interact with another

With the intention of helping him
or her to prosper

Situations will be changed.

Encourage another's talent,

Encourage another's unique
personality,

Praise another's achievements

And, by focusing on these aspects,

Help to bring forth that person's qualities.

In so doing,

You are not only helping someone else,

But also

Allowing your own good qualities to flourish.

Whilst it remains important

To make the most of any encounter,

No meeting happens accidentally.

And, in order to harness the potential

Of every encounter,

You must first accept the
other person

Just as he or she is

With willingness.

Fail to keep an open mind,

And you will not be able
to accept

Anything wholly as it is.

To accept others

Is

To accept your True Self.

To allow others to flourish

Is

To allow your True Self to flourish.

14

What kind of wishes do you
nurture

Now?

Surely, you must have various dreams

That are not so difficult to achieve?

And yet,

It is also wonderful

To cherish dreams

That may require a couple of years
to be realised;

Or,

To foster a huge ambition

Which may take several decades to be
fulfilled.

Whatever your wishes and your desires,

The key is

To imagine them as clearly and
realistically as possible.

Picture them vividly,

Visualise them colourfully.

For instance,

If you have desires such as,

'I want to become happy',
'I want to get married',

'I want to change my job', 'I want to
move to a new place',

Bring them into focus.

Ask yourself: when, where, with whom?

Or with what kind of person?

What kind of things do you want to do together? and

What kind of relationship do you want to enjoy?

Utilise your feelings and emotions fully.

Talk about your desires, write them down, and visualise them ...

Affirm them powerfully to the Universe.

The important thing is

To believe in them completely like a child,

To experience them vividly,

And

To allow joy and enthusiasm

To spring forth from within.

15

Do not cling to visible reality.

Do not judge people only by their words and actions.

All things are engaged in a process of transition, and

Every person is in the process of changing and evolving.

You must not judge things by logic and reason alone.

As you calm your mind, you will
come to know the truth.

This moment, now, is always
the best time.

This moment, now, always offers the
best opportunity.

But only if you believe this,

Only if you relate to this moment
earnestly,

Will the things necessary for you
occur

As if they had just been waiting
to happen.

Know that you can make
your life flow.

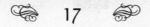

17

Express what you feel and what you think.

If you are not able to
love yourself,

You will live life in endurance,
compromising with others.

To express yourself honestly is

To respect yourself and
others too.

Sincere communication is the key to living life freely.

God bestowed freedom upon every person, and is watching us.

Are you not

Holding on to something now?

Whether conscious of it or not,

We often hold on to,

Or

Are attached to, some particular thing.

When you feel somewhat gloomy,

When you cannot calm your anger,

When you are so ashamed of yourself

That you feel like running away;

When you are deprived of your
confidence by fear,

Sit yourself down, then

Open and stretch the palm of
your mind,

And

Observe it calmly for a while.

You will realise what

You are holding on to.

Past failures, anger, bitter feelings
of regret,

A strict sense of values, prejudices,
worries about the future.

It may be someone you like,
your family;

Stability, wealth, a sense of pride
or lost youth.

When people hold on to something stubbornly,

They are unable to act naturally and become distressed.

They cannot live freely and lightly.

Free yourself from attachment, and empty your mind.

Have a little more courage

In order to become someone

Who can receive infinitely
all that is new.

19

We are all given hurdles

In order to stretch ourselves.

The hurdle may vary

From a petty daily concern

To a crucial matter of life or death.

Even if it is small, it does not mean
that it is easy to overcome.

Even if it is big, it does not mean that
it is impossible to overcome.

It may be

A habit that has to be broken, or

A message that is difficult to convey, or

A taxing problem that needs to be solved, or

A cherished dream that hasn't yet come true.

Whatever it is,

Know that you are not given problems

That you cannot overcome.

It is your wavering mind

That determines your limitations

By presuming

What is impossible, what is beyond
your capabilities,

What is unbearable.

Stop being a perfectionist,

And become an optimist instead.

Try to overcome your difficulties with
a relaxed mind.

As you tackle your problems one by
one,

You will discover the keys to solving
them.

You will also gain confidence.

And then

Help and support from the great
Universe

Will arrive in many forms,

Along with the message that,

'You don't have to shoulder it all on
your own.'

20

Flowers express loveliness,

Trees easiness,

Mountains steadfastness,

The sky open-mindedness,

The great ocean freedom,

The earth abundance,

Animals uniqueness,

And

The sun benevolence.

What do you want to express?

We are gifted with infinite ways

With which to express ourselves.

Through speaking, through writing,
through creating,

Through acting, through dancing,
through singing, through painting;

When you express yourself
just as you are,

You are also increasing your happiness.

Leave your stubbornness, pride and
shyness aside

For a while.

As long as you keep worrying about
your reputation, or

If you are always concerned about the
reaction of others,

You will not allow your True Self to
come forth;

You will not allow your wonderful
potential to blossom.

Say 'okay' to yourself just as you are.

Pure-hearted expression creates
harmony with others

And

Honest expression brings bouquets of
love.

21

Do you remember

How you received many blessings

When you were born into this world?

God, the great Source of life, blessed
you,

Bountiful nature sent you blessings,

And

Your parents and the family you chose
blessed you.

Therefore,

You are able to live your entire life

As one who is truly blessed.

Whenever it is,

Whatever it is,

Whoever it is,

If you relate to it with a mind
brimming with blessings,

You will be treating yourself lovingly at the same time.

You will be experiencing noble love.

Bless the happiness and success of others;

Bless the victories, beauty and cleverness of others

Unconditionally.

Bless every part of your life

Unconditionally.

Even experiences of hardship, failure, grief or despair,

And

Even towards those who are troublesome, aggressive or annoying;

Without blame, without criticism, without being disheartened,

You can, at least, direct your thoughts
so as to bless them, and

Therein springs the fountain of
powerful love

That transforms all positively.

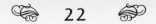 **22**

Humour is a kind of magic

That can transform your life into a
cloudless blue sky.

When you laugh like an innocent child,

Your body and mind are healed.

How many times have you laughed
today?

Have a proper laugh every day.

As you become able to observe things

With a relaxed mind and humour,

You will also be able to laugh off the
hard things

And transform them into sources of
power.

Rather than talking so much,
remain silent.

Rather than thinking too much, tune
into your feelings.

Untroubled and

At ease,

Try to wait without making a move.

Try to trust without making
a decision.

You alone create your reality.

No one else can be blamed for it,

Nor does it exist for the sake of
anyone else.

Through facing every kind of reality,

Through discovering every aspect of
yourself,

You will learn, love and nurture
yourself infinitely.

live this life courageously and
positively.

25

Do you like to change your image often?

For instance,

By having your hair cut
dramatically short,

Or

By wearing a different colour than
you usually do?

Enjoy a casual attitude to change.

For

Change may even refresh your mind.

It may be difficult, though,

To change your job, your home or
habits,

And it is almost impossible

To change other people's thoughts or
values,

Their attitudes or lifestyle.

Still, you set a good example to them.

Your positive transformation

Will be an encouragement to others.

God has given us a good example in
the Laws of Nature:

The exquisiteness of the four changing
seasons;

The rich variety of trees, flowers and
animals;

The mystical wonders of the clouds,
the sky, the moon,

The sun, the earth, mountains and
oceans.

This very moment is bursting with the
joy of transformation.

Even if you suffer today, your pain will
not last forever.

Even if you are joyful today, your
delight will not last forever.

Rather than clinging on to all that you
see,

Live fully in this very moment, now.

Change is none other than the process

Through which we constantly
transform ourselves, and progress.

As you rise courageously to the
challenge of change,

Change will spread its wings around
you.

And then,

The Universe will offer its support to
you.

26

It is often said, 'Saying is easy,
but doing is difficult.'

We all know the truth of this.

'All right, I'll do it!'

– We can very easily say.

Yet,

When the time comes for action,

We may lose enthusiasm,

Or end up leaving the job unfinished.

Therefore, begin with the tasks you enjoy:

Do something you want to do.

For a while, put aside excuses such as:

'I don't have enough money',

'I don't have enough time',

'I am too old for that kind of thing'.

Your True Self is an active person.

If you truly want to do it,

The means can always be found.

As you continue to do what
you enjoy,

You will begin to find that even
difficult things

And things that you are
not very good at

Become more interesting.

And then, the energy to deal with
challenges

Will flow forth from within.

You are the only one who can spur
yourself into action,

And also the one to carry out the task.

As you take one step forward, the flow
will increase.

When you act with joy and
enthusiasm,

You will become a stranger to
weariness.

For

Divine wisdom will naturally support
you

In many ways.

27

Life is filled with many opportunities

And the freedom to choose
between them.

Every day,

You make many choices on many matters.

It also is your choice

Whether you follow the voice of your
True Self,

Or whether

You obey your doubts, your fears,

The opinions of your parents, friends,
or other influences.

You simply want to take note

Of the consequences of your
choices.

Success, failure, wealth, poverty, health
and even illness –

All show you how you have used your
energy.

None of them are good, bad, right or
wrong in themselves.

Now,

Observe this reality and, from here
onwards,

Will you choose to aim towards a
higher goal?

Will you choose to use this
opportunity for major growth?

It is, of course, your own choice.

It is important,

Without clinging to what is superficial

Or fretting about the opinions of
others,

To search for the messages hidden
within you.

Everything depends on how you
receive them

And how you respond to them.

If you choose love, courage and hope,

With gratitude,

It is never too late to start life anew.

The starting point is always 'now'.

Your freedom to choose is a blessing
from Heaven.

28

If you cannot believe in others,

It is because you do not believe in
yourself.

If you cannot believe in success,

It is because you do not believe in
your potential.

If you cannot believe in happiness,

It is because you do not believe in
your creative power.

The power to believe

Is

The gift of love

From the great Source of life.

You are completely free to use it how
you will.

Never place your faith

In misfortune, failure, incompetence,
loneliness or weakness.

Believing in

Happiness, success, talent, friendship,
health and creative power

Will afford you a positive outlook.

Your present situation

Merely shows you clearly

What you have believed in until now.

You are the only person

Who can direct your power of faith

Towards that which is fortunate,
truthful and beautiful.

When you practise this with pure-
hearted faith,

You will come to know the truth that

The gift of love you receive will
become more plentiful

And more abundant.

Gently opening your mind,

Listen to the voice of truth.

It may come to you as an inspiration.

However small its whisper,

Heed it and accept it.

Taking note of the voice deep within

Serves as a guide to the happiness

Of living in harmony with your True Self.

Like a small child, let your eyes
sparkle, and

Challenge all things with a playful
mind.

Enjoy all things like a child,

Who does not even fear new
experiences.

Any situation can be changed

Depending on how you handle it.

If you enjoy this moment,

Your future skies will be clear.

Whatever it concerns,
you must not hasten towards
a result.

Instead, savour the process fully.

The good or bad of the matter will be
revealed in time.

All things happen by necessity.

Even if it does not go as you
would wish,

———⚬⚬⚬———

You will learn a lot from it.

As you remove the narrow limits of your mind,

The possibilities will increase.

32

You may not always be able to accomplish

Every task smoothly and quickly.

No matter how hard you try, or what you do,

Sometimes, your actions may have unexpected results.

When things do not go to plan,

Bravely face the truth and ⌣

Search out the cause.

Try not to act emotionally,

Or judge events only from their
outcome;

Nor come down on others or
yourself harshly.

Even if you cannot redress the balance
immediately,

Do not worry.

Simply leave your body to the healing
power of abundant nature.

Every event has significance

And

Is what is needed for your
present self.

As you face what has happened with
a light and grateful mind,

It will illuminate your future brightly.

Offer an apology pure-heartedly,

Reflect calmly,

Praise yourself for what you have done,

Fill your mind with delightful
thoughts,

Or

See, listen to and touch beautiful
things.

Healing is a cradle through which you are renewed.

Healing is as nutritious as mother's milk.

33

Giving a present;

Offering a helping hand;

Suggesting some good advice.

Do you enjoy giving something to others?

Giving certainly is a virtue.

Yet, reflect for a moment:

Do you feel awkward when you ask for help, or ⌒

On receiving, or if looked after by
another?

Not wanting to be any trouble;
perhaps your pride cannot accept it, or

Not wishing to rely on others; feeling
ashamed, or

Not willing to put any pressure on
others ...

But then, how would you feel

If you were to offer

A present, an act of kindness, a gesture
of love,

And

If this were to be rejected,

Or received with hesitation?

'Giving' and

'Receiving'

Are both virtues of an equal value.

Receiving

With open-mindedness

And

With gratitude

Brings happiness

To both you and the other.

34

If there is someone you cannot forgive,

If there is something you cannot forgive,

If you cannot forgive yourself,

You cannot experience true happiness.

Nor can you know the flow of true life.

For

The Source of life

Is love reinforced by unconditional
forgiveness.

It is not that there really is someone
who cannot be forgiven,

Nor that there really is something that
cannot be forgiven,

Nor that there really is something
about you that cannot be forgiven,

But,

Because you have an attitude that
allows no forgiveness,

You have become unable to
feel love.

When you get angry,

When you want to blame,

When you are disheartened,

These are the best opportunities to
practise 'unconditional forgiveness'.

Open your arms and embrace
everything.

This is your chance to make great
progress

Through savouring true happiness.

For

This is what your True Self wants you
to do.

Forgiveness from the bottom
of your heart

Will heal all the elements of the other
person and of yourself.

Forgiveness is a wonderful magic,
changing despair into joy.

35

Baking a cake and inviting friends
for tea;

Throwing a party and having people over –

What delightful activities these are!

Well then,

What would you like to invite into
your life?

In accordance with the Law of
the Universe,

———— ⚬⚬⚬ ————

You can invite every person you want,

Every event you wish for, everything
you desire.

In accordance with the Law of the
Universe,

You can invite what you need, what is
useful to you,

What is akin to you.

For instance,

Say that you try hard to befriend
another,

Yet you are betrayed or fall out with
each other;

Or, say that you do all you can to
succeed,

Yet your efforts are not appreciated
and you are disappointed –

The cause for this may be hidden
within you.

For instance,

It may be that,

Because you embrace fear or anxiety

Deep within your mind,

You are attracting

Fearful and anxious situations

Unconsciously.

In order to invite

What you truly wish to invite into
your life,

Carefully observe the state of your
mind.

36

Trust in love that overflows
in your mind.

Trust in God that resides in your
mind.

Relax your body and mind and,

Accepting all aspects of yourself just
as they are,

Let go of your attachment and free
yourself.

As your mind fills with gratitude
and joy,

Your agony will disappear.

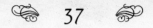

37

Nature is full of awakenings
and healings.

The radiance of the sun, the song of
birds,

The colour of flowers, the scent of
trees;

The whispering wind, the consolation
of the stars,

The murmuring of rivers, the
playfulness of clouds.

All things in the Universe are brimming
with the breath of God.

You are as filled with this as you are
open to it.

You have never been alone.

You have always been connected to the great Source of life.

In the past, present and even in the future,

From morning, at midday and even midnight,

You are enfolded in and supported by limitless love ⟿

———❧———

Without which you simply wouldn't
be alive.

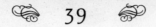

39

We are blessed

With the talent of enjoyment.

Everyone, as a child,

Displays an abundance of this talent

Pure-heartedly, innocently and freely.

Yet how about as grown-ups?

However wonderful your talent,

If you do not use it, it will become
rusty.

There is no age-limit

To enjoyment.

It has nothing to do with age,

Or place or time.

In poverty, endeavour to cope,

In wealth, learn to share with others,

In loneliness, discover things you can
do alone,

In pain, strive to overcome.

As you try to enjoy all that life offers,

Open-mindedness, humour

And wisdom will flow for you.

And then,

Many other talents

Will emerge.

In addition,

You will experience the joy of
attracting

More abundant joy.

40

How was your day today?

At the end of each day,

Allow yourself a peaceful moment.

If your day passed peacefully,

Offer thanks for this,

And

If you feel tense and strained,

Take care of your body and mind

So that you can unwind.

Finding a peaceful moment

Should be included

In your daily routine

Just like washing your face, changing your clothes,

Tidying up, preparing meals, or having a shower.

Even if you are extremely busy,

Give yourself at least ten or twenty
minutes in which to relax.

Then, when you can, take more time –
even a few hours.

Relaxation time is important

In order to perpetuate your energy,

In order to feel like your True Self,

In order to receive healing,

And ⌒

In order to stay calm.

Just as flowers and plants need water
and light every day,

Relaxation is a gift to your life

That only you can give to yourself.

41

You have constantly been given, and are continually being given, even now,

All that you need,

All that is necessary for you,

All that is instructive to you,

All that inspires you.

You are also given

Opportunities

To give

What you have

To someone else

For good reason.

At times, it may be money or goods.

At times, it may be compassion, praise
or encouragement.

At times, it may be labour, a helping
hand or your time.

At times, it may be your knowledge,
ideas or talents.

Whatever it is,

Anything you give to others

Is an act of love.

Love offered with joy

Never diminishes.

The more you give, the more
it flows.

Offer to others

That which has been given to you

By the great Source of life

And then,

Such is the law of repercussion,

You will receive even more plentifully

As your reward.

42

We often talk of

Observing the scenery,

Observing the flowers

Or

Observing the stars.

Well then,

Other than observing

Your shape in the mirror,

Do you ever reflect upon
and observe

Your mind, your actions, your words,
your emotions?

When you make a habit of

Observing consciously and purposefully

The actions you have taken and the
swell of your emotions,

You will be rewarded with

Inner enlightenment.

Remember, though,

That which is observed in those moments

Must be seen through the mind's eye of your True Self.

Awaken your True Self,

Which is able to observe reality as it really is –

Beyond emotion, judgement, thought
and criticism.

Doing so

Is the quickest way

To find true happiness.

43

Every day, you create your life anew.

You never create the same thing today
as you did yesterday.

If you think this is just another day
like the one before,

It will turn out to be just another day
like the one before,

But if you change, the situation will
also change.

How and what you change all depend
on your choices.

Happiness and success depend on your
sincere faith and actions.

Always be aware of yourself –

What you are feeling now,

What you are thinking now, what you
are saying now.

Without being swayed by the reactions
of others,

Without worrying about what others
will think of you,

Consciously allow yourself to be
just as you are.

And love yourself all the more for it.

45

With a tolerant mind, forgive the errors and mistakes of others

Caused by their immaturity –

Even their rudeness, their betrayals

Their unreasonableness and their slanders.

Do not judge them nor be hurt by them.

Do not blame them nor grieve.

Tears shed in forgiveness create

A shower of purification and blessings.

Within a forgiving mind, springs a
fountain of love

And Divinity shines forth.

46

Every person is an artist.

For we all create every aspect of
our reality

Through the power of our minds,
thoughts and actions.

Only some of us are aware of
this truth,

Whilst others are not.

To which group do you belong?

Those who are not aware of it

Sleepwalk through reality.

Even if they believe they have achieved
something,

The results of their efforts may appear

Far removed from their intentions,

And therefore,

They cannot accept what they have
created for themselves.

Instead,

They come to believe that

Someone else or even fate

Has forced such a reality on them,

And continue to repeat actions

That cannot lead them to satisfaction.

Open wide your mind's eye and look!

In the process of creation,

Lies your learning, progress and joy.

As long as you live with this
awareness,

You can create a new reality.

Knowing that you are the
master of your destiny

Affords you

Easiness

And

Freedom.

We, ourselves, are the creations of God.

Let's savour the process of creating our unique work.

47

How do you feel this very moment?

Whatever your feeling, accept it.

Savour it deeply.

Without judging, analysing, oppressing,

Simply focus your awareness onto the self who is feeling it.

Try to imagine that

You are opening wide a window in
your house:

Light streams in at once;

The wandering wind will greet you.

Footsteps and voices, the laughter of
children,

Scents of trees and flowers,
birdsong,

The aroma of good cooking, sounds of
construction work –

What else comes in through your
open window?

Take a slow, deep breath and

Learn how to focus your awareness

Onto your body and heart.

Do not let a moment go past unaware,

But feel it.

Align yourself with your True Self.

As you become more aware, an
awakening will occur.

Forget others and the outside world
for a while.

What your True Self seeks

Is

To be one with abundant love.

48

Being flexible

Towards events

Is

A good thing.

With rigid thoughts, a rigid mind, a rigid body,

With hard words, a hard face, a hard attitude,

Nothing will go smoothly.

Flexibility

Decreases disputes,

And

Affords freedom.

It prevents people

From clashing with each other,

And from getting hurt.

In this wide world,

There are many people with different
ways of thinking,

With different tastes, with different
views,

From different worlds.

And this is what makes Earth so
interesting and exciting.

If you always stick to your own way
of thinking,

To your own tastes, to your own views,

To your own frame of references, even if unconsciously,

You limit yourself to a life within narrow boundaries.

You deprive yourself of opportunity and the joy

Of learning different things

From different people in this wide world.

The human being is primarily a free being

With flexible thoughts, a flexible mind
and a flexible body

Flowing like wind, like water and
like light.

To recover your flexible self

Is

To recover every kind of possibility.

It is to restore the happiness of living
naturally.

49

Befriending and becoming intimate with our True Selves

Is the most important goal in life.

Deep within yourself,

Resides your True Self

Who is serene and overflowing with infinite possibility.

However,

You must become aware of this Self,
and

Endeavour to communicate with it

Pure-heartedly and earnestly.

'A doubting self', 'a merry self",

'A striving self,' 'an excited self',

'A stubborn self', 'a blaming self',

'A thinking self', 'a regretful self',

'An impatient self', 'a depressed self' –

Such selves that change all the time

Do not constitute your True Self.

Your True Self overflows

With wisdom and boundless love, and

Simply exists, never changing.

Your True Self never leaves you.

Merge into one with your True Self,
which resides closest to you, and

Which is your inner reflection of God,
your soul.

This self is a source of answers to your
every question,

Of guidance, and of love and power.

Simply befriend it and become one
with it.

Your True Self is eternal, at one with
all existence.

50

There are things you can
understand by listening calmly.

There are things you can learn by
observing carefully.

Like a small child,

Open your mind pure-heartedly.

If you feel it fully, awakening will occur.

If you savour it fully, enlightenment
will come.

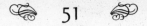

51

Y ou may love, yet if you worry

Or feel distressed or uneasy,

It is time for you to observe your love
calmly.

Are you not expecting too much?

Are you not lacking confidence and
trust?

On the pathway towards true love,
there are many passing points.

Genuine love accepts all and affords
you peacefulness.

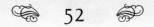

52

Do not jump to hasty decisions, judging good or bad.

If you are swayed by your emotions,

You will miss what is truly precious.

Enter gently into your inner depths, your True Self.

Spend moments and days in calm.

Connect with your Divine Self that resides deep within.

Truth is always revealed from
deep within.

53

Even though

We may not consciously act in this
way,

We often run away from things

Without our realising it.

We find many excuses for our
behaviour:

Too busy, too difficult, simply
impossible;

It's not my job; I can't deal with him or her;

It's not the right time; there's no money;

Someone else can do it better; I have no confidence;

I don't want to cause any trouble; I can't do it alone;

I don't know how; it will resolve itself, and so forth ...

Yet, do remember,

The things that happen to you

Are only those things that concern
you.

The harder,

The more unpleasant,

And

The more difficult it is for you
to deal with,

The more worthwhile it is for you to face it now.

Because,

Even if you run away now,

It will come back to you one day, without fail,

Perhaps in a different guise,

To remind you that you once ran away.

Therefore,

Resolve it now, and be renewed.

54

Amongst all forms of happiness,

Nothing exceeds the bliss of

Your body and soul being filled

With overflowing gratitude.

Once you have experienced this,

You will be able to transform

Every agony and pain in your life

Into happiness, through gratitude.

You can take the first step

This very moment.

Whatever your reality now,

Whatever your state of mind now,

You can still murmur simply,

'Thank you.'

Even if your mind does not agree,

Do not worry,

And

Try to repeat, like singing a song,

Or

Chanting a mantra:

'Thank you, thank you,

Thank you so much.'

Let these words flow from within and
fill you.

Then, these words will leap forth and
spread into the world.

Your present happiness will continue
to increase.

Your present agony will flee through
the door of awakening.

Your True Self knows

How precious your life is, just as it is.

Use the power of these words, of
'thank you', as a tool for
transformation.

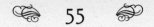

55

Everyone suffers.

Even if you pretend not to,

You cannot deceive yourself.

The more serious and unselfish your suffering,

The harder you have to search for its cause,

To discover it, and learn from it;

And through this

The stronger you will become.

There is nothing worthless, meaningless
or useless

In your life.

(Although you, yourself, may deem it

Worthless, meaningless or useless.)

After all, you have always tried your
very best,

Haven't you?

Suffering represents a process

That encourages your independence,

And nurtures your confidence.

The important thing is

Not to dwell on it too long,

But

To search for a way out.

If you continue to sit in the dark pit
of your problems,

No one else can offer you light.

Yet your own hand can kindle

Sparks and light in your mind.

As soon as you begin to seek your way out,

Even if you are feeling your way,

The helping hand of the great Guide
will be waiting for you.

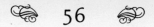

56

Is there something in which

Your mind is entangled right now?

If there is, try to discover what it is.

It may be a small matter,

Or

It may be a huge matter.

Many troubles may drift around
your mind.

If this is the case, place them in their
order of priority.

The key is to deal with the one

That requires the most urgency.

Without postponing,

Without offering excuses,

Determine to deal with it anyhow.

You may observe it calmly,

Or

You may contemplate it.

But

Do not lay the responsibility for it on others!

Do not blame yourself!

Do not worry unnecessarily!

Do your best, with a positive attitude.

It doesn't matter if you can only do little now.

Start with what you can do

And,

Having done your very best, relax.

Trust the result to the hand of Heaven;

For

Heaven knows all about you.

Therefore,

The matter will surely be resolved in the way

That is best for your present self.

57

You are a unique being,
different from anyone else.

Therefore, you should never compare
yourself with others.

Do not judge yourself as inferior in
comparison with others!

Do not judge yourself as superior in
comparison with others!

If you respect your personality,
your inner light will shine forth,

Which will then grow into respect for
all other people.

There is no adversity that you cannot overcome.

There is no experience that has nothing to offer you.

For your inner wisdom

Knows your capabilities.

However thick and heavy the wall

Presented by a new experience,

Beyond it lies a path

That can lead you towards infinite
happiness.

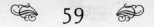

59

If you are striving for happiness and success,

Have complete faith and yearn for these passionately.

Loosen all your attachments to past failures or setbacks.

Negative thoughts such as discomfort, fear and doubt

Are heavy shackles that hinder you

From stepping forward.

If you crave for happiness and success,

Anticipate these with enthusiasm.

Step forward with a light heart,
focusing on your new dream.

60

With any issue,

It is important to deal with it calmly.

Even if it only involves a small

And simple matter,

It is a lost opportunity

If you underestimate it and

Deal with it superficially.

For

Everything that happens around you

Is a test provided for your growth,

Whether at a beginner's level, an
intermediate level

Or an advanced level.

If you cannot get high marks in your
daily tests,

How will you ever be able to get a high
mark in an important test

Such as a final examination or an
entrance exam?

In this way,

The small events of daily life

Are the preparation

You need to become someone who,

When tackling bigger problems,

Is able to fulfil his or her mission
resolutely

257

Without being seized by panic.

Every chore, obstacle or problem

Serves you as a springboard for growth.

Therefore,

Keep calm in your daily life

To enable you to tackle every kind of event.

61

Have you ever thought

How important it is

To behave kindly in minor matters?

It is often very difficult to tackle big issues

With kindness.

Therefore,

Try to be kind towards the people around you,

Or

When dealing with everyday details.

When you give water to your potted plant;

When you play with your cat or dog;

When you talk to your father or mother;

When you speak to your friends over the phone;

When you write a thank-you letter –

Anything will do.

Just be a little kinder

In the actions of your daily life.

The more that kindness is drawn forth

From the well of your mind,

The more it will gush forth of its own accord.

As it becomes more and more
plentiful,

You will be able to bring great
kindness

To difficult situations

And

In times of hardship

And

Even to those of whom you are not
very fond.

Such kindness creates a path to true
happiness.

62

Even if you keep quiet and do
not speak out,

Your thoughts affect

Your whole body and your entire soul.

Even if unseen by your eyes,

Your thoughts spread throughout
the world.

Be conscious of the power
of thought.

If you cherish thoughts

That are gentle, beautiful and
righteous,

That are joyous, progressive and
generous,

And that are positive and lively,

They will embody themselves in your
reality

Because they have power.

Whereas,

If you embrace negative, dark thoughts

That are fearful, irritable and
miserable,

That are depressive, discouraging,
hateful,

These too will become manifest in
your reality

Because they also have power.

Open the window and let a new
breeze flow in,

Sort out your problems and be
refreshed,

Wash out the dirt and welcome in
pleasantness,

And

Polish and give a good shine to your
mind.

That which eliminates darkness

Is

The light of bright thought.

You are the only person

Who can switch it on.

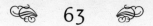

63

When did you last

Offer a gift,

Not to another,

But to yourself?

Give at least one gift to yourself

Each day.

It certainly is such a delight

At times

To reward yourself

With a gorgeous present.

However,

In your daily life,

By simply broadening your
perspective,

You can discover plentiful gifts

Even in

Small things, invisible things or
humble things.

Enjoy exercising your kindness

By finding and devising a gift

For yourself.

Take more time for your skin care,

Discover a new way to wear a scarf,

Decorate a room with your favourite
flowers,

Prepare a tasty lunch box,

Give yourself some praise,

Change the interior of your living space,

Spare the time to enjoy nature,

Talk with your old friends over the phone –

One lovely gift each day!

Savour the joy

Of giving to your self

And

Of receiving.

Where on Earth is God?

He resides deep within you.

He has always been and

Shall always be.

God is with you.

He is merging into you.

Everyone lives searching for love.

For love is the very source of life.

Offer love.

Receive love.

Do not fear to give love –

There is no one who is not worthy of receiving love.

When you are tired, bathe your whole body

In the golden brilliance of the sun.

When you feel lonely, go to the fields and mountains

And rest yourself in the greenery and flowers.

Nature overflows with a peacefulness that offers

The gifts of love and healing.

When you are in pain, play with water
and wash it away.

When you are at a loss, listen to the
song of birds

And the whispering of the wind.

67

You must not fret about

Working for others.

For it isn't that

You are being employed by

A particular person or company,

So much as that

An unseen power wishes and is
attempting

To make you grow

Through that particular person or
company.

Know that it is the plan of Heaven,

And try to fulfil your task.

Then observe

How much difference your new
attitude makes,

Compared to working reluctantly.

First of all,

You will notice the enhanced results of

Your efforts.

Your relationship with your employer
or company

Will change,

And then,

New radiance will emerge

In your mind.

Possessions, money and status

Do not bring true joy.

Eternal joy cannot be granted by those,

But can only be earned by changing
your attitude.

68

Your mind is filled
with joy...

What does this mean?

Is it because

Your wish has come true?

Or that

An unexpected event has taken place?

Or that

You have had a delightful experience?

Or that

You have received praise?

When joy ripples through your mind
like waves,

Your body will also rejoice vibrantly.

Your eyes and skin will become
radiant.

You will act more freely.

Anything you do will go smoothly.

Therefore,

Whenever it is,

Whatever it is,

Always enjoy finding ways to reap joy.

Even if it concerns only a
small matter,

Or

However hard it may be,

If you embrace it with joy,

Your enthusiasm for life will be
increased.

And,

As your joy spreads outwards,

Touching other people and your
surroundings,

Joy will continually bear more joy.

And then,

All that you have given the world

Will grow into a surprisingly

Immense new cause of joy,

And

Come back to you.

69

It is very important

To seek clarity in all that you do.

If, fearing to know the truth,

You leave matters ambiguous,

Or

Lacking confidence,

You leave them unsettled,

You are simply seeking to escape.

However,

You must not attempt to seek clarity

Dictated by the concerns of others

Or situations in the outside world.

Do not worry about the reactions

Of your surroundings,

And, instead,

Calm your mind and observe with your
mind's eye;

Open your mind and listen with your
inner ear;

And ask your True Self for clarity.

In order to be clear about exactly who
you are,

Observe every emotion and every
thought.

In order to meet your True Self,

Spare enough time for this.

What are your true feelings?

What do you truly want to do?

Who do you truly love?

What are you truly striving for?

The answers from your True Self

Will come to you one day without fail.

70

Cultivate the open-mindedness

That resides within you.

It is wasteful indeed

To spend your precious time and energy fruitlessly

By, for instance,

Continually regretting what has already been done, or

Constantly repressing anger, or

Worrying about the future.

In those moments,

You would do better to detach your
thoughts calmly

From the object or person at the root
of your problem

For a while,

And

Try to direct your body, eyes and mind
towards Nature,

Which pure-heartedly displays

The open-mindedness of God's love:

Winds blowing breezily,

Large trees standing calmly,

Birds singing lovely songs,

Mountains resting in dignity, ⁓

The brilliantly shining sun,

The leisurely flowing rivers.

Humankind is also a child of Mother
Nature.

To be unshackled from attachment

And

To cultivate open-mindedness

Is to be natural.

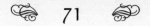

71

What do you wish from the bottom of your heart?

What is it that makes you animated?

The answer resides within you.

Talk to God, who resides within you.

Trust in the mystic power inherent within you,

You who are blessed to be alive.

The power that can bring happiness to
you already resides

Within you.

Whatever the situation, each
and every encounter

Is caused by necessity.

An encounter represents an
opportunity to know your own truth.

Deep within each encounter afforded
you, a blessing lies and

The opportunity to grow as much as
you can is concealed.

You will encounter every kind of
people, event and reality.

Encounters create a seven-coloured
rainbow

That can enrich your life.

73

Your body is a vessel with
which to express your mind.

Be gentle with it, especially when you
are tired, stressed or ill.

If you treat your entire body lovingly,

Your heart will open and be healed.

If you cherish you body, your body will
rejoice and be revitalised.

We all need to offer love and
refreshment to our bodies and minds.

Are you on good terms

With your intuition?

Everyone, at one time or another,

Has an intuitive glimmer

Without special reason or special
cause,

Even, sometimes, without realising it.

Such intuitive glimmers may arrive

In various ways,

Like a wind blowing gently,

Like soft sunlight breaking through the
clouds,

Like the delicate scent of flowers,

Like beautiful birdsong,

Like a sudden flash of lightning.

If your mind is pure and open,

You will catch them.

An intuitive glimmer is a message

From your True Self

Who knows all.

As you cherish and make use of it,

It will be a trustworthy messenger,
bringing good guidance.

When you follow your glimmers of
intuition,

You unite

The innocence of a child with the
wisdom of an adult.

75

Are you familiar with skipping, the children's game?

The rope is low in the beginning and,

As children jump without getting tangled in it,

They raise the height gradually.

Pole-vaulting and hurdles are similar sports.

Just as in such games and sports, ⌒

We too can quickly raise the standards
we set in life.

To use our talent not only for
ourselves

But more widely for others and society

Is a mission filled with joy.

In order to achieve this,

We need to strive positively

To overcome our limitations.

Instead of comparing yourself
with others,

Or

Being affected by outcomes,

You have only to overcome

The limitations set by your own mind.

Study, work, love, marriage,
relationships,

Beauty, health, personality, habits,

hobbies, thoughts, emotions –

Aim to raise the standards in every
aspect of your life.

The energy and love granted by the
Source of life

Are infinite.

If you use them fully,

Nothing will be impossible for you.

76

You are never alone, even for
one single moment.

Even if you do not have a good friend,
lover,

Partner or children at present,

You must realise that

It is because

You have chosen to live this way ⌁

In order to learn first how to connect

With your precious True Self.

If you appreciate this,

You may, therefore, be better off on
your own for now.

You can learn a lot this way and still
enjoy life.

And yet, remember that,

Whenever and always,

Your True Self is firmly connected to

The great Source of life.

It is always connected to

The great Source of love.

You are connected to all of the world.

Therefore,

Whenever you take delight,

Whenever you learn and grow,

The world also takes delight,

Also learns and grows.

When you love yourself,

All things that are connected to you

Are also loved.

There is no reason to worry:

Live simply in the awareness of this
connection.

77

Indeed, every kind of incident
occurs in life.

And not all are pleasant or
exciting.

Unpleasant things and even
disappointments

Can happen to you and be yours.

However,

Always remember that

You are a courageous adventurer who
has come to this Earth

In order to discover the real happiness

That your True Self yearns for.

If you cannot remember this,

Simply accept this reality:

All that happens in your life

Has been chosen and accepted by your
True Self,

Who continually wishes to grow.

The drama of your life unfolds

With the events and details that are

Necessary to your present self.

There is no such thing as failure or
a mistake.

Accept that events do not happen
by chance
And ignite your latent potential.

In what kind of adventure story

Would you like to cast yourself
as the hero?

78

Having done what you
had to do,

Now you must not worry about the
result

Or trouble your thoughts with the
opinions of others.

Trust all to the flow of Nature;

Allow yourself to drift along with a
peaceful mind.

Having done all you could do, with
enthusiasm and sincerity,

The important conclusion now

Is to believe and have complete trust.

 **79**

When anger, fear, uneasiness
or worry arise,

Do not be swayed by these emotions
nor suppress them.

Without blaming anyone else for them,

Accept them bravely.

Every emotion you experience

Reflects the energy of you, yourself.

If you savour these feelings

Without rejecting or detesting them,

Healing will take place.

In this moment,
feel how happy you are.

In this moment, choose to be
grateful.

This very moment means
everything to you.

This very moment is your only chance.

Whatever your reality in this moment,
your mind is free.

You cannot live other than in this
moment.

Always and more than
anything else,

Love yourself.

Regardless of the state of your present
self,

Regardless of what you have
experienced in your past,

You too are a student in the process of

Growing constantly ⟶

In pursuit of happiness.

Love does not know

Comparisons, conditions or
limitations.

To nurture yourself with self-respect

While accepting yourself just as you
are now,

And to embrace yourself warmly

Is

To love yourself.

To love yourself

Is

To love your life, which you create,

To love all those to whom you are
connected,

And

To love all things in the world that are
connected to you.

You are nourished through ceaselessly
receiving

Abundant love from the great Source
of life.

And why not!

You can surely love even those you are
not very fond of,

And

Even those who have betrayed you.

Your True Self and everyone else's
True Self

All wish to reside in sublime love.

Your pure prayer

Becomes a serene light

And

Is delivered to Heaven.

Your prayer of gratitude

Becomes a beautiful light

And

Is delivered to Heaven.

Your prayer for betterment

Becomes a bright light

And

Is delivered to Heaven.

Your compassionate prayer

Becomes a warm light

And

Is delivered to Heaven.

Your devoted prayer

Becomes a great light

And

Is delivered to Heaven.

Prayer

Is a bridge

That connects

You and Heaven.

When your prayer is filled with trust,

And you continue to act bravely,

Heaven will respond with a powerful light,

And

Always illuminate your way,

And guide you.

Heaven will always send you
encouragement

And embrace you with eternal love.

ABOUT THE AUTHOR

Juan Nakamori was born in Tokyo, Japan.
Looking up at the sky one day, she had a
vision of a multitude of angels filling the
heavens. Since then, the angel messages that
she has received have filled readers around
the world with love and encouragement.